ELLIE SIMMONDS

CHAMPION SWIMMER

Clive Gifford

WAYLAND

First published in 2013 by Wayland

Copyright © Wayland 2013

Wayland
338 Euston Road
London NW1 3BH

Wayland Australia
Level 17/207 Kent Street
Sydney, NSW 2000

Editor: Nicola Edwards
Design: Basement68

A catalogue record for this book is
available from the British Library

ISBN: 978 0 7502 7800 3

Printed in China

Wayland is a division of
Hachette Children's Books,
an Hachette UK company.

www.hachette.co.uk

Picture acknowledgements:
The author and publisher would like
to thank the following for allowing
their pictures to be reproduced in
this publication:
Cover: AP Photo/Alastair Grant; p4 Lynne
Cameron/PA Wire; p5 AP Photo/Alastair
Grant; p6 Stefan Rousseau/PA Wire; p7
Steve Parsons/PA Wire; p8 Tom Shaw/
Getty Images; p9 Barry Batchelor/PA
Wire; p10 Ben Birchall/PA Wire; p11 David
Jones/PA Wire; p12 Anna Gowthorpe/PA
Wire; p13 Getty Images; p14 AP Photo/
Greg Baker; p15 Julien Behal/PA Wire;
p16 David Davies/PA Wire; p17 Johnny
Green/PA; p18 Anna Gowthorpe/PA Wire;
p19 Lynne Cameron/PA Wire; p20 Getty
Images; p21 Getty Images For LOCOG;
p22 Getty Images; p23 Sean Dempsey/
PA Wire; p24 Getty Images; p25 AP
Photo/Alastair Grant; p26 Featureflash /
Shutterstock.com; p27 Paul Gilham/PA
Wire; p28 PA Wire; p29 Ian West/PA Wire

Contents

Paralympic glory

September 1st 2012: tension mounts inside the Aquatics Centre at the 2012 London **Paralympics**. Some 17,500 spectators are ready for what they hope will be a gripping S6 400m **freestyle** swimming race. Most eyes are on **lane** 4, where Ellie Simmonds, with her red cap and goggles on early, is shaking her arms, preparing for her crucial race.

INSPIRATION

Ellie was hugely inspired by the large, supportive crowd at the Aquatic Centre. After the race she said, "It's my **home Games** and in front of my home crowd and all my friends. It's definitely one of my best. It's definitely one of my highlights. The crowd gave me everything."

Ellie had **qualified** fastest of the swimmers who'd reached the final. Her time that morning for eight lengths of the 50-metre pool was a stunning 5 minutes, 24.64 seconds. It was the fastest ever time at the Paralympics and a European record. It was also Ellie's **personal best**. Yet, she feared her excellent **form** would not be enough, for she was up against the one woman who had swum faster – Victoria Arlen of the United States. Arlen was the world record holder with a time 0.18 seconds faster than Ellie's best.

Ellie swims strongly during the 400m S6 Paralympic freestyle final. At this stage in the race her rival, Victoria Arlen (left), is just ahead of her.

As the **starter's** pistol fired and the eight swimmers dived into the water, the Aquatics Centre erupted into noise. Within 50m, four swimmers had pulled away from the others with Ellie in fourth place, but after 200m, Ellie and Victoria Arlen were more than 10m ahead. The two 17-year-olds battled hard, with Arlen holding the lead until Ellie surged as they turned to race their final length.

Ellie powered onward to extend her lead and touch first – she had won gold! She pounded the water with delight and burst into tears. Her time of 5 minutes, 19.17 seconds smashed the world record by over five seconds. It was an astonishing performance. Ellie Simmonds had been under great pressure as the female face of the London Paralympics – and she had delivered.

INSPIRATION

Ellie was spurred on to success by her friendly rivalry with Victoria Arlen. Speaking after the race, Ellie said that Arlen, "pushed me to the best of my abilities and that was great for me, we were neck-and-neck and the crowd was going mental, and that gets everyone excited in Paralympic sport."

Ellie clutches her gold medal and posy of flowers proudly as she stands on the podium at the 2012 Paralympics. It was an amazing moment for the young British swimmer.

Small, that's all

On 11th November, 1994, Val and Steve Simmonds welcomed their fifth child into the world. They named her Eleanor and still call her that today, though the rest of the world knows her as Ellie. By the time she was born, two of her three sisters and her brother, Stephen, had grown up. So Ellie was brought up with her sister, Katie, who is seven years older than her.

While their three older siblings are all of average height, both Ellie and Katie were born with **achondroplasia**. This is a form of dwarfism that occurs in around 1 in 25,000 people. It results in short bones in the arms and legs, which means that an adult with this condition is usually between 1.2 and 1.3m tall.

Steve and Val Simmonds wear special Ellie t-shirts as they support their daughter at the heats for the S6 400m freestyle.

INSPIRATION

Ellie's parents have always been a massive source of support and helped build her positive attitude. In a 2012 interview with *Fabulous* magazine, Ellie noted, "They always treated me like I'm just a normal person. They said if I wanted to achieve something I shouldn't let it stop me."

Apart from providing raised stools so that the sisters could reach light switches and table surfaces, Ellie and Katie's parents tried not to treat the girls any differently from their older siblings. And Ellie certainly doesn't think of herself as restricted in any way. In a 2012 interview with *Radio Times* magazine, she said, "I've never really thought of myself as disabled. I'm just a normal person, but a bit smaller than everyone else... I don't think of myself as that different. I'm just the same inside."

Ellie's father worked as an environmental consultant and the family initially lived in a house in Sutton Coldfield in the West Midlands. Ellie remembers her early childhood fondly. Even at a very early age, she preferred to be active, taking ballet lessons and playing with friends in her large garden. Ellie loved taking part in athletics events at school and showed a competitive streak that would serve her well in her swimming career.

WOW!

Ellie auditioned for the role of a giant in a school play at Cooper and Jordan Primary School in Aldridge. She got the part!

Ellie hugs her niece, six-year-old Molly, on her arrival back at Heathrow Airport after the 2008 Beijing Paralympics. Team GB won 42 gold medals at the Games.

Into the pool

The Simmonds family's first house included an outdoor swimming pool – a rare luxury in Britain. As soon as Ellie was allowed in the pool, she was rarely out of it. She enjoyed learning to paddle and splashing around with friends. By the time the family moved to Aldridge, Ellie had grown to love life in the pool and had started having weekly swimming lessons.

At first she didn't like putting her head in the water, but the **coaches** encouraged her to build her confidence and soon she was swimming up and down the pool, sometimes with her older sister, Katie. Ellie loved the element of competition right from the start, working hard to keep up with her much older sister or children of normal height.

Nyree Lewis celebrates winning the women's 100m backstroke S6 competition at the 2004 Athens Paralympics.

INSPIRATION

Ellie watched the 2004 Athens Paralympic Games on television. She was enthralled by the gold-medal-winning performance of British Paralympian swimmer, Nyree Lewis, and vowed to match her achievements.

Before Ellie had turned eight, she was invited to take part in twice-a-week swimming sessions at Boldmere Swimming Club in Sutton Coldfield. There, she swam against children of her own age but of normal height and received coaching to help her improve her strokes. There are four different strokes in competition swimming: **front crawl, back crawl, breaststroke** and **butterfly.** Ellie learned and worked hard to improve all her strokes.

Ellie was eight when she swam in her first race at a swimming gala. She came last but that didn't deter her. Quite the opposite. She was thrilled to have been selected and loved every element of the day, from taking part in races to cheering on her teammates. She began swimming even more often after school, and by the age of ten was taking part in four or five training sessions a week, as well as competing regularly.

TOP TIP

It's natural to feel a bit nervous when you're learning to swim in a big pool. Ellie did. But if you stick with it and listen to your teacher or coach, you're bound to improve.

Ellie stands next to her hero, Nyree Lewis, at a celebration in Cardiff in 2008 for Paralympians from Wales.

Making sacrifices

Ellie was just ten when she competed in her first British Junior swimming championships. She won all her races in the under-14s category. Everyone could see she showed real promise and she was asked to join UK Sport's World Class Talent programme. She was the youngest member of this group of sportspeople with the potential to win Olympic or Paralympic gold medals.

Ellie was taking swimming really seriously now, but was struggling to get enough time in the pool to train properly. Her local pool was often crowded, preventing her from sprinting down a lane. She also needed more advanced coaching to compete at higher levels in disabled sport. Billy Pye was a swimming coach who specialised in Ellie's S6 classification of disabled swimming, but he was based in Swansea some 240km away from Ellie's home. Ellie started visiting Billy at half terms and in school holidays.

WOW!

Ellie's coach Billy won the Welsh Coach of the Year award in 2008, beating Warren Gatland, the head coach of Wales' grand-slam-winning rugby union team.

Billy Pye (right), who coached Ellie to win Paralympic gold, was a former coal miner who retrained as a primary school teacher and top-flight disability swimming coach.

Billy spotted immediately that Ellie had immense talent that he could help to shape. This led, when Ellie was 12, to the Simmonds family making a momentous decision to split into two. Ellie and her mother would move down to Swansea during the week and come back to the family home at weekends. In her book, *Swimming The Dream*, Ellie wrote, "it was really hard because I had to leave my old friends, my old club and my dad...I knew straight away that it was the best thing for my swimming, so that made it easier."

Moving to Swansea wasn't the only major upheaval in Ellie's pre-teen life. As she was growing, Ellie's legs were bowing (curving outwards). This is a common problem for people born with achondroplasia and, in Ellie's case, could be corrected with surgery. At 12 years of age, Ellie had four metal plates inserted in her legs. She had to use a **zimmer frame** to help her walk in the months afterwards. Yet, just three weeks after the operation, she was back in the pool, using just her arms to swim.

After her 2008 Paralympic triumph, Ellie went back to Olchfa School in Swansea to celebrate with her friends. The warm friendships she forged at school were a strong source of support during her early career.

TOP TIP

Don't give up on a swimming stroke if you struggle with it. At first, Ellie's best strokes were butterfly and breaststroke. Now, she counts front crawl, used in freestyle races, as her best stroke.

In competition

In disabled sport, athletes are grouped in classifications so that they compete fairly against each other. There are ten different classifications for swimmers with a physical disability from S1 (the most severe) to S10 (the least). Athletes with different disabilities may be placed in the same group. Ellie is an S6 swimmer, a group for those with dwarfism but which is also for athletes who have lost two limbs or have no useful leg muscles.

TOP TIP

Ellie always tries to stay positive and learn from the races she doesn't win. Performances of rivals help spur her on in training to do her best.

In April 2006, Ellie was thrilled to take part in her first British Championships at Ponds Forge in Sheffield. She didn't qualify for the final of the 100m freestyle race but came second in the 400m freestyle. In December, Ellie flew to Durban in South Africa. She had just turned 12, making her **eligible** to compete at her first International Paralympic Committee (IPC) World Championships.

Medal-winners in an S6 category event at the 2012 Paralympics. Ellie holds her bronze medal alongside Dutch swimming legend Mirjam de Koning-Peper (centre) and Victoria Arlen from the US (left), who won silver.

Despite being the youngest member of the squad, Ellie wasn't **overawed** by the experience. Her parents flew out to the competition as well but she barely saw them as she hung out with the GB team, watched others compete and enjoyed being surrounded by **elite** athletes from all over the world.

In the pool, Ellie was overwhelmed by the power and experience of rival competitors and finished last in the 50m butterfly final. In the 400m freestyle event, Ellie finished fifth but knocked almost 30 seconds off the time she swam at the British Championships earlier in the year. What's more, she took part in the final alongside her idol, Nyree Lewis, who won the event.

WOW!

In November 2007, swimming in a **short course 400m** freestyle race, Ellie broke her first ever world record, swimming a time of 5 minutes, 51.19 seconds.

Ellie powers through the water at her first ever World Championships as she competes in the 50m butterfly event. She was just 12 years old at the time.

Ellie's first Paralympics

Ellie thought that competing at the 2006 World Championships was part of the journey towards making her Paralympic **debut** at London in 2012. So she was amazed to learn that coaches and experts were tipping her to appear at the Beijing Paralympics four years before that. At the 2008 British Championships Ellie qualified for the 2008 Paralympics by setting a new world record time of 5 minutes, 48.26 seconds for the 400m freestyle.

Ellie made the GB Paralympic team and, aged just 13, was the youngest member of the squad in any sport. Excited but nervous, she enjoyed her time in the capital city of China. She shared an apartment with six other GB Paralympic athletes and visited a silk market as well as the world-famous Great Wall of China. However, her races did not begin well. Overcome by nerves before the final of her first event, the 200m **individual medley**, she burst into tears and thought about pulling out. Billy, her coach, helped calm her down and told her to go out and just enjoy the occasion.

Ellie and Mirjam de Koning-Peper hug and look to the scoreboard after their 400m freestyle race at the 2008 Beijing Games.

WOW!

In her record-breaking performance at the 2008 British Championships, Ellie beat her swimming heroine and inspiration, Nyree Lewis.

Ellie was disappointed with her fifth place but the nerves were banished and she vowed to do better in her next event, the 100m freestyle. She found herself up against the world record holder in the event, 39-year-old Mirjam de Koning-Peper from the Netherlands. Ellie was just a third of her age but surged past her to win her first ever Paralympic gold medal. In an interview afterwards, Ellie said, "I was determined to get a medal. I didn't mind which colour. In the last 25m we were all in a line and I just put my head down and went for it."

Six days later, Ellie was back in the pool battling and beating De Koning-Peper again into second place. Ellie had won her second Paralympic gold medal, this time in the 400m freestyle. It was a stunning achievement.

Ellie waves to the crowd at the Beijing Aquatics Centre after winning a gold medal at the 2008 Paralympics. In an interview with the BBC, Ellie said, "To stand on that podium is the best feeling in the world."

WOW!
Ellie was the second-youngest athlete ever to compete for Great Britain at a Paralympics.

Dealing with fame

Ellie may have left for China as a relative unknown but, following her performances at the Games, she returned home a hero. In an interview in *The Telegraph* newspaper in 2011, she reflected on the experience, "We had no idea what it was like back home. In the few months after, it really hit home how big it was. I didn't realise how many people had been watching it."

Ellie holds her BBC Young Sports Personality of the Year award. Millions of television viewers watched the ceremony.

Back in England, Ellie found herself snowed under with requests for appearances and interviews. She was awarded life membership of her first swimming club and appeared on several TV shows, including Blue Peter. Her success really struck her when she was nominated for the BBC Young Sports Personality of the Year award alongside tennis star Laura Robson and diver Tom Daley. Ellie won and was presented with the award by boxer Ricky Hatton and footballer Theo Walcott.

INSPIRATION

Ellie is a huge fan of Michael Phelps, the Olympic swimming star. Her coach met him in the United States and brought her back a signed swimming cap. Ellie keeps it in a drawer as she feels it's too precious to wear!

Two months after the BBC award, Ellie found herself at Buckingham Palace where she would become the youngest person ever to be made an MBE (Member of the British Empire). She had to keep the award a secret before it was announced in the New Year's Honours List, but at the ceremony she wasn't alone as her coach, Billy, was receiving an MBE as well. Ellie was extremely nervous about making a mistake and moments before meeting the Queen even slipped out of her high-heeled shoes and put on a pair of flat shoes so she wouldn't fall over!

Ellie has had to learn to cope with her celebrity. She found it quite hard at first always to have to put on a happy, positive face whenever she was spotted in the street, even when she was tired or having a bad day. Writing in her book, *Swimming The Dream*, Ellie stated, "I don't always want to be noticed. Sometimes, I like to keep myself to myself and that's much harder now."

Ellie meets Queen Elizabeth II at Buckingham Palace to receive her MBE. Ellie said afterwards that her heart was beating faster and the faster as the Queen approached her.

WOW!

In 2009 Ellie took part in the TV game show All-Star Family Fortunes with Billy Pye, her brother, Stephen, and her aunt and cousin. Ellie's team won over £1,500 for charity.

In training

To be a top swimmer, you have to train frequently. Ellie trains every Monday, Wednesday, Friday and Saturday morning and usually five or six afternoons or evenings every week. Only Sunday is a complete rest day. Training days start early for Ellie. She usually has to get out of bed by 5.15am to be in the pool for a 6am start. Getting up early is Ellie's least favourite part of her day.

Morning training involves a two-hour session in the pool. These mostly focus on building and **honing** her swimming strokes so they are as accurate as possible. During a morning session, Ellie might swim 3, 500m, which also helps build her all-round fitness and **stamina**. Training sessions later in the day involve series of short sprints in the pool to help build speed as well as exercises out of the pool to strengthen key body parts such as her shoulder joint muscles.

Ellie dives into the pool at the start of a training session. She spends long periods stretching all her muscles to prevent injuries and to help her body perform at its best.

INSPIRATION

Ellie finds inspiration in other swimmers who train and push her to perform better. In the run-up to the 2012 Games, Ellie's training partner was Paralympic triple bronze medallist, Matt Whorwood.

The sessions are long but Ellie knows how to fight off boredom. She told the Wellcome Trust Blog in 2012, "While I'm swimming, I think about what I am going to be doing the rest of the day or sing songs in my head…Training keeps me busy, which I like, but it's also fun and I have made lots of friends through it."

At just 1.23m tall, Ellie doesn't have the **advantage** of long arms and legs to power through the water like some of her swimming rivals. She manages to compete, and often win, by swimming more strokes per minute than others – 120 strokes per minute in the last 50m of her 400m freestyle final at the London Paralympics. This is an astonishing stroke rate in a long race like the 400m. To put it into perspective, the winner of the 400m freestyle in the Olympics, Camille Muffat from France, swam around 80 strokes per minute. To achieve such a rate has taken Ellie a phenomenal amount of hard training.

TOP TIP

Like most successful athletes, Ellie tries to eat a healthy, balanced diet every day, making sure it contains plenty of fresh fruit and vegetables.

Using a snorkel in training can help improve technique, body position and lung capacity. Ellie always pushes herself hard. As she says, "The motto at my training pool is: 'Coming second is not an option'."

Building on Beijing

Beijing was a real high point for Ellie but getting back into training afterwards proved difficult. She needed all her reserves of energy and motivation to push herself hard through the winter training so that she could compete at her best in the following season. What was more, from being the underdog, Ellie was now the girl to beat. Rival swimmers were more determined than ever to defeat her in races.

Ellie started the 2009 season well and at the British Championships in March, set a world record in the 200m freestyle in 2 minutes, 43.85 seconds.

She struck gold again at the European Championships held in Iceland with five victories, including in the 200m individual medley.

Ellie looks at the clock to check her winning time after the 400m freestyle final at the 2009 British Gas Swimming Championships in Sheffield.

WOW!

In a BBC interview, Ellie picked as her fantasy dinner guests: dancer Louie Spence because he makes her laugh, nature film maker David Attenborough for his amazing stories, and actor, Ryan Gosling... "because he is good looking".

In November, 2009, Ellie flew to Rio de Janeiro in Brazil for the first ever IPC World Short Course Swimming Championships. This featured races over the same distances as the Paralympics or regular World Championships, but all held in a 25m long pool, half the length of a normal competition pool. Ellie was stretched as she was taking part in seven different events. Astonishingly, she won six of them and gained a silver in the other, the 100m individual medley. Propelled by Ellie's performances, Team GB finished fifth on the medal table with 17 golds. Ellie had won over a third of them!

Ellie carried her brilliant swimming form into 2010 with success at the 2010 World Championships held in Eindhoven, the Netherlands, with two silvers and a bronze in three relay races (where teams of four swimmers swim, one at a time) and four gold medals in individual races.

HONOURS BOARD

IPC World Championships

2 competitions entered (2006, 2010)
Medals won: 4 gold, 2 silver, 1 bronze

IPC European Championships

2 competitions entered (2009 and 2011)
Medals won: 7 gold, 1 silver, 1 bronze

Ellie poses with track athlete Christine Ohuruogu (right) and TV presenters, Adrian Chiles and Christine Bleakley, representing the Paralympics at the launch of the London 2012 ticket website.

www.tickets.london2012.com

Lloyds TSB
Supporting your journey to London 2012

A day in the life of Ellie Simmonds

Much of Ellie's time is spent either studying or training and competing. Ellie spent many years at Olchfa Comprehensive School in Swansea (see page 11), where she was a popular pupil and had many friends. She maintains that they rarely mentioned swimming, preferring school gossip and talking about music and celebrities – one of her favourites being Justin Bieber.

In 2011, Ellie sat exams and gained nine GCSEs in Maths, English, Double Science, History, Child Care, Food Technology, Sport and Welsh. Her results in her AS levels the following year weren't as good as she'd hoped, although she received a C grade in World Development. In 2013, she continued to study for her History AS level with a tutor at home.

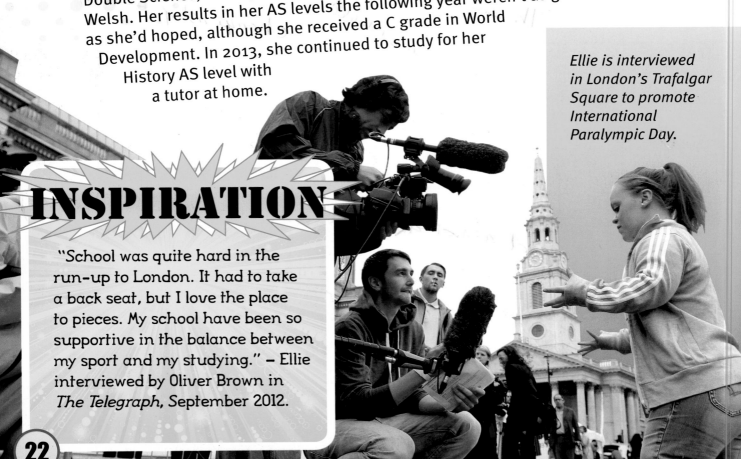

Ellie is interviewed in London's Trafalgar Square to promote International Paralympic Day.

INSPIRATION

"School was quite hard in the run-up to London. It had to take a back seat, but I love the place to pieces. My school have been so supportive in the balance between my sport and my studying." – Ellie interviewed by Oliver Brown in *The Telegraph*, September 2012.

Away from education, Ellie's high profile as a sportswoman means she is often asked for media interviews, photoshoots and to attend events organised by her sponsors, such as Adidas and Cadbury. The car company BMW gave Ellie a Mini One hatchback car specially adapted for her with a raised floor and extended foot pedals. In March 2012, Ellie passed her driving test and the car gives her the freedom to get around. It also means that her mum, Val, doesn't have to act as a taxi driver all the time!

When she has time off, Ellie may take a 'pyjama day' hanging out at home watching TV. Shopping for clothes and shoes and cooking are some of her favourite pastimes. Ellie cooks for her mum most Thursday nights when they are in Swansea. Ellie particularly loves baking cakes and pastries and says she's the 'team baker' for her swimming squad.

Ellie takes part a line up of Team GB stars, including Tom Daley, Louis Smith and triathletes Alistair and Jonny Brownlee, at the launch of BMW's plans to support the 2012 Olympics and Paralympics.

WOW!

In 2013 Ellie was the joint winner when her baking skills were put to the test on TV in the Great Comic Relief Bake Off.

320d
EfficientDynamics

Second time around

By the time London 2012 came round, Ellie, despite being a teenager, was an experienced, race-hardened competitor. She was promoted as the poster girl of the GB Paralympic Team, literally, as a gigantic poster of her covered an entire wall of the Westfield Shopping Centre next to the Olympic Park. After an exciting and successful Olympics, Ellie was expected to deliver at the Paralympics held 17 days later.

Ellie looks pensive and tense as she enters the London Aquatics Centre and waves to her fans shortly before racing at the 2012 Paralympics.

Ellie laughed off the poster in pre-Games interviews but the pressure was mounting. She had lost races in 2011 to her close rival, Mirjam de Koning-Peper, while Victoria Arlen from the US was the world record holder in Ellie's two favoured events, the 100m and 400m freestyle.

Ellie put aside fear of failure to win her first event, the 400m freestyle, in style (see pages 4-5). She followed with a bronze in the 50m freestyle, an impressive achievement. This sprint down a single length of the pool tends to favour taller swimmers.

INSPIRATION

Ellie wore headphones as she walked out to the Paralympics pool on which she listened to Eminem's *Lose Yourself* before her races. For her first final, the 400m freestyle, she took one earpiece out as her coach had suggested she listen to the noise of the home crowd.

The 100m freestyle had been Ellie's strongest event in the past and at the 2012 Paralympics she swam a personal best, one second faster than ever before. But Victoria Arlen was after revenge and pipped Ellie to the gold medal.

Shortly before the 100m freestyle, Ellie had swum a sensational race in the final of the 200m individual medley. She was in sixth place early on and still over two seconds behind the leader, Oksana Khrul, as they turned for the last length of the pool but powered ahead with her freestyle stroke. Ellie's teammate, Natalie Jones, lost the silver by 1/100th of a second but Ellie won gold by almost nine seconds and in a new world record time.

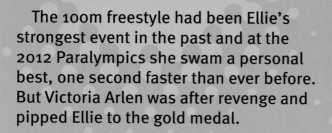

WOW!

Ellie produced personal bests in all four of her events at the 2012 Paralympics – proof that she had trained hard and well for the Games.

A beaming Ellie shows her joy and relief after winning gold at the 2012 Games. She now has bronze, silver and gold Paralympic medals which she jokes are very heavy to wear all at the same time.

After the Games

Ellie declared the London 2012 Paralympics "the most amazing two weeks of my life" and really didn't want the Games to end. She took part in the closing ceremony, and with Paralympic 100m sprint champion, Jonnie Peacock, lit a torch from the Olympic cauldron shortly before it was put out. Ellie really missed the Paralympics in the months that followed but was kept busy dealing with a packed social diary.

Ellie went on TV and radio, starred in a parade in her home town of Aldridge where her old primary school, Cooper and Jordan, named their swimming pool after her, and opened new or renovated swimming pools across the country. She was invited to fashion shows, parties and film premieres, nominated for BBC Sports Personality of the Year and won a number of other awards including The *Sunday Times* Young Paralympian of the Year.

Ellie on the red carpet at the premiere of the James Bond film Skyfall in London in 2012.

WOW!

A plaque put up in Ellie's honour in Birmingham in 2012 to celebrate her achievements spelled her surname as Simmons. It was soon corrected!

In many interviews, Ellie has said that she doesn't see herself as a swimmer forever, but speaking after London 2012, she was uncertain about what the future will hold. She began studying in order to re-take exams and for her future career, has thought about public relations, going to university and even working in a bakery or patisserie.

Ellie returned to the pool near the end of 2012 for serious training. She has used other sports and taken Zumba fitness classes to build her speed and stamina up again. Her first major target was the 2013 World Championships in Canada. The next Paralympics will be in the Brazilian city of Rio de Janeiro in 2016 and Ellie has said that her goal is to be there.

WOW!

To commemorate her two gold medals at the 2012 games, the Royal Mail painted two letter boxes gold, one in Swansea and one in her home town of Aldridge.

Ellie waves to the crowds who gathered to watch the London 2012 victory parade for members of the GB Olympic and Paralympic teams.

The impact of Ellie Simmonds

Ellie Simmonds is a phenomenal sportswoman who has won multiple British, European and World championships. She has four Paralympic and ten World Championship gold medals to her name, all won while she was still in her teens. She has set and held numerous swimming world records.

Ellie's feats in the pool have won her a legion of fans and inspired others to take up swimming, either for fun or to take part in competitions.

These include Amy Marren, who was just ten years old when she watched Ellie win at the 2008 Beijing Games. Four years later, Amy made it into the GB Paralympic swimming team alongside Ellie and said, "I still get star-struck around her."

INSPIRATION

Opening a new swimming pool in London in 2012, Ellie said, "I love meeting kids. It's great to be an inspiration for the next generation...I would tell them the first thing is to enjoy what they do... Give everything you've got and always try your best at everything." – *Ellie in the Islington Tribune*, November 2012.

A blindfolded Ellie tries her hand at goalball at the Lee Valley Athletics Centre as part of an initiative to get more children of all abilities into sport.

A firm believer in a healthy active lifestyle, Ellie has taken part in several major schemes to increase the number of children and teenagers playing sport for fun, fitness and to build confidence. Ellie also supports a number of charities, including the Dwarf Sports Association, which aims to make sports available for people of all abilities who have restricted growth.

Ellie's fame and impact extends well beyond the sport of swimming. She is a **role model** for all young people, as witnessed, for example, by being named the Inspirational Hero of 2012 at the Radio 1 Teen Awards. As one of the most recognisable Paralympic athletes, she is playing her part in changing public attitudes to people with disabilities. Her 'can do' attitude to challenges and her insistence that she's a regular person just a bit shorter than average, has given a powerful positive message to others.

INSPIRATION

"Ellie turns up and delivers every time she gets in the pool and it's fantastic how that inspires not only those in swimming but also outside of it."
– Marc Woods, four-time Paralympic swimming champion, BBC Sport website.

On stage at the Wembley Arena, Ellie accepts her 'Inspirational Hero of 2012' award at the Radio 1 Teen Awards. Her success and personality have impressed children and adults alike.

Have you got what it takes to be a champion swimmer?

1) Do you play sports that require high levels of fitness such as long-distance running, cycling or energetic team sports like football or netball?
a) Yes, I play lots of sports and love a really hard workout.
b) I am neither fit or unfit. I only occasionally play energetic sports.
c) No, I prefer watching sport or playing computer games to playing sport.

2) How often do you go swimming?
a) I visit my local pool regularly and swim lengths there when I can.
b) I go now and then in the school holidays and occasionally at weekends.
c) Only on holiday and then I mostly muck around in the pool rather than swim.

3) Are you very competitive when playing sports or games?
a) I hate losing and try to improve so that I don't lose the next time.
b) I'd prefer to win, but if I don't I shrug my shoulders and forget about it.
c) I don't mind who wins.

4) How well can you swim?
a) I can swim well but would love to improve and learn how to swim all the strokes.
b) I can just about swim one or two lengths and am not that interested in learning other swimming strokes.
c) I can't swim or I can only swim a few strokes before I have to put my feet down.

5) Are you good at concentrating on things for long periods of time?
a) Yes, I can be very single-minded and focused on a single task.
b) Sometimes, but my mind does tend to wander a bit.
c) I get bored easily with one thing as I'm interested in lots of things.

6) Are you prepared to sacrifice your social life to train long, long hours?
a) Yes, if the goal, such as being a competition swimmer, was worth it.
b) I'm happy to do some training but still want plenty of leisure time with my friends.
c) No. I don't like the sound of lots of training at all.

RESULTS

Mostly As: You may just be cut out for competition swimming. Why not ask your PE teacher or at your local swimming pool about taking part in a local swimming club's junior sessions?

Mostly Bs: It doesn't sound like you're ready to swim competitively, not yet at least. Why not try some casual races with friends or see if you can improve your swimming strokes?

Mostly Cs: Swimming seriously may not be for you but knowing how to swim a length or two of a pool is a useful skill to have. Why not pop down to your local pool soon?

Glossary

achondroplasia A form of dwarfism that occurs in around 1 in 25,000 people. It results in short bones in the arms and legs.

advantage A position of superiority over someone else.

back crawl A swimming stroke in which you lie on your back and kick your legs up and down while sweeping each arm overhead and then through the water.

breaststroke A swimming stroke performed on your front with your arms making circular sweeping movements and your legs kicking with a pushing action.

butterfly A swimming stroke performed face down with both your arms sweeping over your head at the same time.

coaches Training or fitness advisors.

debut First appearance or performance, for example on stage or at a competition.

eligible Satisfying the rules or conditions for entry to something, such as being old enough to compete in a race.

elite Describes people who are the best in their field, such as swimming or athletics.

form Physical condition or fitness.

freestyle Races or events which allow you to swim using any stroke you chose. This is usually front crawl as it is the fastest swimming stroke.

front crawl A powerful swimming stroke in which you swim on your front and make long sweeping strokes of your arms while kicking with your legs.

home Games An Olympic Games that takes place in a competitor's own country.

honing Working to improve something, aiming to make it as good as it can be.

individual medley An event in which one competitor swims separate parts of the race using all four major strokes: backstroke, breaststroke, butterfly and freestyle.

lane A marked out narrow corridor in a swimming pool down which a competitor swims in a race.

overawed Intimidated and made nervous by something or someone.

Paralympics The major sports competition for top athletes with a disability which takes place once every four years in the weeks after an Olympic Games.

personal best A swimmer's best ever time for a certain swimming stroke and distance.

qualified Made it through to the next round of the competition.

role model A successful person in sport or some other field. The way that person behaves is often copied by others, especially young people.

short course Races held in swimming pools which measure 25 metres in length.

stamina The ability to keep working or exercising for a long time.

starter The official who begins a race with a signal, such as firing a starting pistol.

zimmer frame A metal frame with four legs that people can use to support them if they have difficulty walking.

Index

INSPIRATIONAL LIVES

Contents of new titles in the series

Tom Daley
978 0 7502 7999 4

Diving superstar
Taking the plunge
Conquering fears
Beating the adults
Early setbacks
Back on top
First Olympics
World beater
Darkest days
London looms
Olympic hero
A day in the life of Tom Daley
The impact of Tom Daley
Have you got what it takes
  to be a world-beating diver?

Jessica Ennis
978 0 7502 7998 7

The world's greatest all-rounder
Early potential
A growing medal collection
Senior breakthrough
Injury nightmare
On top of the world
A winning habit
Joy turns to anxiety
Back on track
Golden girl
Honouring a champion
A day in the life of Jessica Ennis
The impact of Jessica Ennis
Have you got what it takes
  to be an Olympic champion?

Mo Farah
978 0 7502 7996 3

Mighty Mo
Growing up in Africa
A new start
Schoolboy champion
Learning his craft
Time to get serious
Tough at the top
Getting faster
On top of the world
Olympic hero
Time to celebrate
A day in the life of Mo Farah
The impact of Mo Farah
Have you got what it takes
  to be a champion runner?

Ellie Simmonds
978 0 7502 7800 3

Paralympic glory
Small, that's all
Into the pool
Making sacrifices
In competition
Ellie's first Paralympics
Dealing with fame
In training
Building on Beijing
A day in the life of Ellie Simmonds
Second time around
After the Games
The impact of Ellie Simmonds
Have you got what it takes
  to be a champion swimmer?

WAYLAND